This Costly Countess - Bess of Hardwick

by

Elizabeth E

ISBN 1-974754 95 X

2001

The Derbyshire Heritage Series

WALK & WRITE LTD
UNIT 1,
MOLYNEUX BUSINESS PARK,
WHITWORTH ROAD, DARLEY DALE,
MATLOCK, DERBYSHIRE.
ENGLAND.
DE4 2HJ

Four times the nuptial bed she warm'd,
And every time so well perform'd,
That when death spoil'd each husband's billing,
He left the widow every shilling.

Horace Walpole 1760

The 400 acre estate which lay between Hardstoft and Ault Hucknall had been farmed by the Hardwicks since the early 14th century. In the reign of Henry VIII the Hall was a modest half-timbered manor house owned by John Hardwick, a man 'of ancient family but diminished fortune'. Here his wife, formerly Elizabeth Leake of Hasland near Chesterfield, gave birth to four daughters and one son before John died in January 1528.

There is no record of their birth dates but the children were evidently healthy enough to survive the hazards of a medieval childhood spent in the bleak climate of north-east Derbyshire.

Their widowed mother, left in impoverished circumstances, struggled to cope with the estate and the upbringing of her family. In John's will he had directed that his daughters should each receive 40 marks (about £26) as a marriage dowry, not a sum likely to attract a husband of rank and an impossible amount to be obtained from the estate.

Mistress Hardwick's financial situation showed no improvement when, after a couple of years, she remarried. Her new husband was Ralph Leche and being a younger son of the owners of Chatsworth he had no expectations. The birth of three daughters did nothing to mitigate their circumstances and it is not surprising that Ralph was imprisoned for debt in 1538.

Many conflicting dates have been suggested for the year that Elizabeth, known as Bess, John Hardwick's third daughter was born. It was probably 1520 or soon afterwards. The custom was, at that time, for children to be brought up by friends or relatives, preferably in a higher social scale, and before Bess was twelve she joined the London household of Lady Zouche, a Derbyshire woman from Codnor Castle who was a relative of the Hardwicks.

There she met young Robert Barlow or Barley from Barlow near Chesterfield and helped to nurse him when he was taken ill with a 'chronical distemper'. As a result, Robert fell in love with her and they were married, but he died shortly afterwards 'before they were bedded for they were of tender years'. Contrary to the report that Bess inherited all her husband's property, she received only the customary widow's portion which amounted to no more than £50 a year.

Nothing more is heard of Bess until 1547 when a memorandum in the diary of Sir William Cavendish, aged forty-two, stated, 'I was married unto Elizabeth Hardwycke my 3rd wife in Leestersheere at Bradgate House the 20th August in the first yeare of Kinge Edward the 6 at 2 of the clock after midnight'.

Bradgate House. Photograph by John N. Merrill

Bradgate House was the home of Henry and Frances Grey, Lord and Lady Dorset, who were the parents of Lady Jane Grey. Bess was probably employed there as a lady-in-waiting. Years later the Duchess of Newcastle who was married to Bess's grandson, wrote that 'Sir William, being somewhat advanced in years, married her for her beauty'. Small and slender with red-gold hair, Bess had a charm and vivacity

4

never revealed by her portraits and Sir William fell completely under her spell.

The second son of a Suffolk squire, he had been a commissioner under King Henry VIII for the dissolution of monasteries, being awarded many properties and lands that had belonged to the abbeys. One of these was the Manor of Northaw in Hertfordshire. In 1546 he received a knighthood and was appointed Treasurer of the King's Chamber, thereby pocketing all revenues from Crown lands.

Bess and her husband divided their time between Northaw and their house in London near St. Paul's Cathedral. Here they enjoyed a lively social life which involved much gambling. The two surviving daughters of Sir William's first marriage lived with them and, within ten years, Bess had produced eight children, two of whom died in infancy.

Their first child, Frances, named after Lady Dorset who was her godmother, was born in 1548. The following year Lady Jane Grey was godmother to their second daughter, Temperance, who lived for only a short time. This was the year in which Sir William was persuaded by Bess to sell his properties in the south of England in order to 'purchase lands in Derbyshire where her kindred lived'. Bess's younger sister, Alice, had married Francis Leche of Chatsworth, son of her stepfather's eldest brother. They sold the estate to Francis Agard who soon found himself unable to find the money for its upkeep and he let Sir William relieve him of it for £600 which included the cost of the house.

At the same time Sir William exchanged his Northaw property for lands at Doveridge and within a few years he also acquired the manor of Ashford near Bakewell. He then bought another 250 acres of land at Chatsworth and Baslow, together with a part of Edensor village which, at that time, stretched down into the river valley. All the estates purchased were in the joint names of William and Elizabeth Cavendish.

In December 1550 their first son, Henry, was born and the Princess Elizabeth, later Queen Elizabeth, was his godmother. Two more sons followed, William in 1551 and Charles in 1553. Then came two daughters, Elizabeth and Mary in 1555 and 1556 and finally a girl called Lucretia who was born and died in 1557.

By this time the Cavendishes occupied a more imposing house in London, situated close to the River Thames. Here they lived extravagantly and, as it turned out, beyond their means, entertaining many guests from Derbyshire including Sir James Foljambe from Walton near Chesterfield, members of the Manners family and Lady Port who had been a Fitzherbert. Bess's mother and her brother James, still at Hardwick, stayed with them frequently.

Dinner for guests was served at 11 a.m. and supper was at 6 in the evening. The meals were accompanied by the music of a harpist and all the servants wore a blue livery. Exotic foods were served and quantities of ale consumed. Sir William regularly drank two pints of wine at dinner and at supper.

While Bess was in London, her mother or her sister, Jane, or sometimes her mother's sister, Marcella Linacre, took charge at Chatsworth and loads of furnishings, hangings and plate were sent from London with directions about the alterations.

'Cause the floors in my bedchamber to be made even', wrote Bess to her steward, 'and all the windows where glass is broken to be mended'.

She kept a note of the expenses incurred, paying a carpenter 8 pence a day and 5 pence a day for his man.

When Mary Tudor ascended the throne, Bess and her husband, as Protestants, kept away from the Catholic court and spent most of their time in Derbyshire. The family lived in some discomfort, however, for Chatsworth House was in a poor state of repair and plans for a new house were being considered.

'I understand you have a cunning plasterer', wrote Sir William to his friend, Sir John Thynne at Longleat, 'I would pray you that I might have him in Derbyshire for my hall is yet unmade'.

The household accounts at this time indicate that there was an abundance of good food to be obtained locally. The gardens produced cherries, pears, apples, walnuts, beans, artichokes and 'cowcumbers'. Butter, eggs, milk and cream came from the dairy while the woods supplied plover and woodcock with sparrows and larks for puddings. When the

Bess of Hardwick in middle age   *Sir William Cavendish*

Sir William St. Loe   *George Talbot. 6th Earl of Shrewsbury*

7

Chatsworth Old Hall

cattle were killed off during the winter months, the family could fall back on venison for the deer were able to survive in the most severe weather.

Sir William travelled to London occasionally but became more and more lax in his duties as Queen's Treasurer until, in 1557, he was called upon to explain a discrepancy in his accounts amounting to £5,000. Sir William admitted neglect but pleaded ill-health and blamed his servants for taking advantage of his 'sykeness'. He begged for clemency for the sake of his 'poore wyfe and miserable and innocent children'.

Bess was already making hasty preparations to travel to London. She set out from Chatsworth on August 27th, 1557, taking with her Henry, aged 6 years and 8 months, and Elizabeth, not quite two and a half.

On the first day the party had to cross the River Trent by ferry at Shardlow and they stayed the night at Loughborough. Here new shoes were bought for two footmen who ran ahead to reserve rooms at each town where they stayed. The second night was spent at Northampton where the horses were re-shod and a pair of shoes, price 8 pence, was bought for little Elizabeth. They reached St. Albans on the third night and, after four days' journeying, arrived in London to find Sir William 'quite undone' and drinking heavily.

Bess realised he was gravely ill and nursed him devotedly, procuring delicacies like oysters and calves' foot jelly to tempt his appetite. All through September he grew increasingly weak and, as winter approached, Bess could only wait for the end. In the diary in which he had entered the details of his marriage to Bess and the births of their children, she wrote, 'Sir William Cavendyshe, Knight, my most deare and well-beloved husband departed this presente life on Mundaie being the 25th daie of October in the yeare of our Lord God 1557'.

Sir William was buried beside his first wife, Margaret, and his mother, Alice, at the church of St. Botolphe in Aldersgate and soon afterwards Bess returned to Chatsworth.

A kindly, generous man, Sir William had made her completely happy and she mourned him sincerely whilst facing a widowhood full of anxiety. With six children of her own and two stepdaughters to bring up, his debt of £5,000 outstanding and money for the purchase of Ashford Manor still to be found, Bess's financial situation looked bleak.

One of the first things she did was to sell the London house, but when Queen Mary died the following year and Queen Elizabeth came to the throne Bess was inclined to spend more time in the capital, and had all her older children with her in rented accommodation for the coronation celebrations, the three boys having had their hair cut for the occasion.

Within a short time, Bess was appointed lady-in-waiting to the queen and was therefore in a position to mix with all the influential people of the realm. Among them was Sir William St. Loe, a widower with children of his own, who was a delicate man 'possessed of divers fair lordships in Gloucester-shire'. He was a staunch supporter of Queen Elizabeth who, soon after her accession, made him Captain of the Guard and Butler to the Royal Household.

Now bordering on middle age, Bess had matured in charm and understanding and the ten years of her marriage had provided her with a confidence born of the exalted position she held in society.

St. Loe fell deeply in love with Bess, although few of her friends could see any attraction in this unprepossessing suitor and Queen Elizabeth was heard to ask, 'Has the woman so far forgotten herself as to marry a common groom?', Bess recognised his unfailing honesty and reliability. They were married in the autumn of 1559 and St. Loe agreed to support not only Bess's own children, paying a portion of the boys' fees at Eton, but also to provide a dowry for one of Sir William Cavendish's daughters. His letters, when they were apart, reveal his affection for 'my sweet Chatsworthe' as he called Bess. 'My owne, more dearer than I am to myselfe,' he wrote to her, 'thine who is wholly and only thine, yea for all time while life lasteth'.

In spite of his court duties St. Loe managed to spend much time with Bess at Chatsworth, incurring the queen's displeasure as a result, and took a keen interest in the new house she was building. Soon after their marriage he was returned as a Member of Parliament for Derby. When the members of his family discovered that he had made a will leaving his estates to Bess outright, they accused her of making 'improper use of her influence' and, on one occasion when she was suddenly taken ill, his brother, Edward, was suspected of poisoning her.

The enforced separations of Bess and her husband came to an end when Bess was appointed a Lady of the Bedchamber. She took her place in the most intimate circles at court and was able to observe, at first hand, the Queen's love affair with Robert Dudley. Another Lady of the Bedchamber was Lady Catherine Grey, sister of the tragic nine-day queen, Jane, and godmother to Bess's daughter, Elizabeth. On 9th August 1561 Catherine impulsively confided to Bess that she had been secretly married to Edward Seymour in the previous November and was now pregnant.

Alarmed and horrified by this news, Bess broke into a 'passion of weeping'. As Catherine and Edward both had royal blood in their veins, the queen's permission should have been sought for their union as their heirs would be in the line of succession. Catherine begged Bess to help her to break the news to the queen but, foreseeing the queen's wrath if her complicity was suspected, she refused to act as an intermediary and the girl, distraught, confessed her secret to Lord Robert Dudley. He immediately informed the queen whose reaction was predictable. In spite of her innocence, Bess was sent to the Tower along with Catherine and Edward whose son was born there on September 24th. 'You shall send for Seyntlow', wrote Queen Elizabeth in a fury to the Lieutenant of the Tower, 'and put her in awe of divers matters confessed by the lady Catherine'.

During her imprisonment Bess occupied comfortable rooms in the Tower, paying 26/8 for her board and lodging, 5/- for the services of a maid and 5/- for fuel and candles. While she was there she communicated with Sir George Pierrepont of Nottingham regarding a marriage between his eldest son, Henry, and her eldest daughter, Frances Cavendish, then aged thirteen. Frances entered her prospective husband's household at Holme Pierrepont as a lady-attendant and Henry paid a visit to the St. Loes in London. Both being found satisfactory, they were married towards the end of 1562 and their son became the first Earl of Kingston-upon-Hull.

Bess was released from the Tower well before the wedding and, before long, her husband's health began to cause her concern. Never a robust man, St. Loe was now aging rapidly and every indisposition he suffered provided his brother, Edward, with an opportunity to spread a rumour that Bess was poisoning him. These charges only made St. Loe more devoted to Bess. He allowed her generous sums of money for the building of Chatsworth and, when the matter of Sir William Cavendish's debt was raised anew, St. Loe paid £1,000 in final settlement.

Sometime at the end of 1564 or the beginning of 1565 Sir William St. Loe died in London and was buried in the church of Great St. Helen in Bishopsgate beside his father. Bess was now a widow for the third time.

Within two years of St. Loe's death there were rumours that Bess was playing the role of a Merry Widow. Henry Jackson, her children's tutor, spread such scandalous reports about her behaviour that Queen Elizabeth ordered an enquiry to be made about his allegations. There is no record of the investigations but Lady St. Loe continued to be made welcome at Court and Her Majesty directed that Jackson should be 'punished with severity that our servant may be restored to her good fame'.

Now in her forties, Bess was not only a physically attractive woman with a remarkable vitality but she had accumulated great wealth from her three marriages. Consequently there was no shortage of suitors for her hand and, before long, one of the richest men in England made her a proposal. He was George Talbot, 6th Earl of Shrewsbury and, many years later, he reminded Bess, 'When you were St. Loo's widow and, to the world, ill-famed and a by-word, I covered these imperfections by my inter-marriage with you'.

Called a 'joyless man', Shrewsbury was the same age as Bess but no match for her intellectually. His deceased wife, who was a sister-in-law of Dorothy Vernon, left him with seven children, one of whom was already married. Captivated by Bess's fascinating personality, he readily agreed to every condition she made concerning the marriages of their respective children. A double wedding was arranged and, on 9th February 1568, in what is now Sheffield Cathedral, Bess's eldest son, Henry, was married to Shrewsbury's eldest daughter, Grace Talbot, and his second son, Gilbert, was married to her youngest daughter, Mary. Because the two brides had not yet reached child-bearing age, Henry and Gilbert were immediately sent off on a tour of Europe.

The date and place of Bess's marriage to the earl, probably late in 1567, has never been established. Her income of about £1,600 a year was transferred to her husband for five years until Henry Cavendish came of age.

Queen Elizabeth was pleased to hear that her 'good old man' had taken such a suitable bride. 'I have been glad to see my Lady Saintlo', she said, 'but now am more desirous to see my Lady Shrewsbury. There is no lady in this land I better love and like'. The Catherine Grey episode was evidently forgotten.

Writing to Bess from London later in the year, Shrewsbury assured her of his affection, 'never tasted so deeply before', and went on to say that the queen was about to bestow on him a rare honour as 'she did trust me as she did few'. This turned out to be the doubtful privilege of acting as custodian to Mary, Queen of Scots, who had fled to England on May 16th after escaping from the Isle of Lochleven where she had been imprisoned. Still under suspicion of having murdered her husband, Darnley, in order to marry Bothwell, she had been forced to abdicate the throne of Scotland in favour of her infant son, James.

Recognising the threat to her own security brought about by this Catholic queen's presence in England, Queen Elizabeth ordered her removal from the northern regions with access to the coast to the midland counties where the Earl of Shrewsbury owned a number of estates.

'Use her honourably but do not allow her to escape', were the queen's instructions and she directed that Shrewsbury should receive his royal prisoner first at Tutbury. Situated on the border of Derbyshire and Staffordshire, the castle there was owned by the Crown and leased by the earl for a hunting lodge.

Tutbury Castle. Photograph by John N. Merrill

Bess began hastily to prepare this cold, damp fortress for the reception of Queen Mary who arrived on 3rd February 1569 in a state of collapse, after a journey of eight days in atrocious weather. Finding the castle uncomfortably bare, Bess had so many 'hangings and other necessaries' transported from Chatsworth and from Shrewsbury's main seat, Sheffield Castle, that she began to complain of 'lacking furniture and lodging for herself'. Silver plate and 'wardrobe stuff' which included tapestries were sent from the Tower of London together with Turkey carpets, silver ewers and four gilt 'chandellours'.

The castle was not large enough to house all Queen Mary's retinue of lords and ladies in waiting, chaplains, physicians, cooks and grooms, and some had to be accommodated in Burton.

Bess was soon on friendly terms with the twenty-seven year old queen whose charm was irresistible and the two ladies spent much time together employed in a common interest — embroidery. The designs for their work were drawn by professional embroiderers who also filled in the backgrounds and mounted the finished pieces. Many of these are now on view at Hardwick Hall, one large panel containing the intertwined initials, MR and ES.

Their friendship caused some concern to the earl for orders had come from Queen Elizabeth that Bess should have contact with the Scottish queen 'but rarely'. Shrewsbury therefore wrote to Cecil, the Secretary of State, assuring him that any conversation between his wife and Queen Mary was 'altogether of indifferent and trifling matters'.

It was not long before Queen Mary began to complain of the coldness and discomfort of her 'miserable little rooms' which she described as 'rather a dungeon for criminals than a habitation fit for a person of my quality'. As for the gardens, she wrote, they were 'fitter to keep pigs in'.

With the coming of Spring, Shrewsbury received permission to move her to Wingfield Manor, a 15th century mansion which stands on a hill overlooking the Amber valley. Queen Mary's apartments afforded a picturesque view across to the village of Ashover and were larger and more comfortable than those at Tutbury but, within a short time, she was taken ill. Two physicians were sent from London but the cause of her sickness, according to Shrewsbury, was the 'uncleanly order of her own folke' who numbered no less than 140 persons. She was therefore removed on a litter to 'Chattesworthe, my wife's hous, eight miles hence' while Wingfield Manor was thoroughly cleansed.

Wingfield Manor © John N. Merrill

Chatsworth House was still in the throes of structural alterations and, after a brief stay, the Scottish queen and her entourage were escorted back to Wingfield. Queen Mary's health had soon improved but now Shrewsbury was taken ill and his son, Lord Talbot, was sent for to take charge of the household. When her husband showed a little improvement, Bess accompanied him to Buxton in order to take the waters.

Queen Elizabeth heard with annoyance that the Earl and Countess of Shrewsbury had deserted their prisoner and left Wingfield without permission and, when she was told of a plot by Leonard Dacre for Queen Mary's escape, she was furious. Orders flew from London to Derbyshire. The Shrewsburys were to leave Buxton at once and proceed to Tutbury and the

Earl of Huntingdon from Ashby-de-la-Zouch was sent to take charge of Queen Mary and return her to Tutbury where 500 extra guards were posted.

For some time plans had been afoot for a marriage between Queen Mary and the Duke of Norfolk. Although she had never met the Protestant duke and regardless of the fact that she was still legally married to Bothwell, Queen Mary was enthusiastic about the proposed union. Aged thirty-three and described as 'no lover knight', Norfolk was said to be the richest man in England and had been married three times before.

Mary Queen of Scots

Queen Mary addressed him in her letters as 'My Norfolk' and wrote, 'You have promised to be mine and I yours. I believe the Queen of England and the country should like of it'. Far from 'liking of it', Queen Elizabeth who was fully informed about their correspondence and exchange of presents, was enraged and had Norfolk arrested.

In October 1569 a Catholic rally in support of the marriage began in the north of England and soon the armies were sweeping southwards. Shrewsbury, now in charge again at

Tutbury, increased the garrison there, had trenches dug and posted scouts to watch nightly. Bess ordered extra quantities of food in readiness for a siege but the Government ordered them to transfer Queen Mary to Coventry. Here, at first, she was lodged at the Bull Inn until accommodation was found for her in a private house. She was strictly guarded and 'never suffered to be seen abroad in any company'.

By February the Catholic armies had disbanded and Queen Mary was taken back to the noisome atmosphere of Tutbury Castle where conditions were more appalling than ever. Noxious smells from the middens pervaded the queen's rooms and she 'wepte and swooned for dayes'. Shrewsbury wrote asking for permission to move her to Chatsworth. 'As the water waxes so evil', he declared, 'so the sickness of the inhabitants will increase'. Eventually he was given consent to move the queen and her party to Chatsworth where they arrived on 24th May 1570.

This was Queen Mary's second visit to Chatsworth where the River Derwent wended its way through the grounds. She was able to ride daily, to walk in the gardens, play bowls and practise archery. She exercised her dogs and rested in a small stone building with a raised garden which is still in existence and is known as 'Queen Mary's bower'. Every day her health improved.

Queen Mary's Bower, Chatsworth.

The cost of building Bess's Chatsworth House, now almost finished, had reached £80,000. Facing east, four storeys high and with four turrets, it was built round a quadrangle. The magnificently furnished rooms were panelled in oak and hung with tapestries. The curtains in Bess's bedroom were of black damask with gold lace edging and the bed cover was in black velvet with a gold fringe.

Queen Mary was lodged in spacious rooms in the east wing, elegantly furnished. The 'Queen of Scots Apartments' in the present house occupy the same site as the suite of rooms in which she stayed as a guest of the Shrewsburys.

While at Chatsworth, Queen Mary was visited by members of several Derbyshire families including the Manners and the Pagets but Queen Elizabeth rebuked Shrewsbury for allowing these visits and accused him of using the Scottish queen as a kind of showpiece.

In the autumn of 1570, Cecil and his wife stayed at Chatsworth for three weeks. The object of his visit was to persuade Queen Mary to renounce her claim to the English throne and to negotiate terms for her possible return to Scotland. No satisfactory decision was reached but Cecil returned to Court with excellent reports of the Earl and Countess of Shrewsbury and their capable guardianship of their royal charge. He also praised Bess's proficiency as a hostess.

In spite of Cecil's opinion that Chatsworth was 'a very mete hous, having no toun or resort where any ambushes might lye', another scheme for Queen Mary's release was devised while she was there. A group of local squires planned to rescue her while she was out riding on the moors and conduct her to the coast. John Beaton, Master of Queen Mary's household, was in the confidence of the four conspirators, one of whom, George Rolleston, betrayed the others and the plot came to nothing. Thomas and Edward Stanley, sons of the Earl of Derby, and Sir Thomas Gerard were arrested and Rolleston was kept for two years in the Tower. John Beaton escaped punishment by dying and was buried in the church at Edensor.

For some time Queen Mary had been involved in a correspondence with the King of Spain by means of a go-between named Ridolfi, an Italian banker who lived in London. Plans were renewed for her marriage with the Duke of Norfolk who had recently been released from prison on the undertaking that he would have no further dealings with Queen Mary. He was soon deeply involved in this new conspiracy which aimed to behead Queen Elizabeth and put Queen Mary on the English throne with Norfolk as her consort. In no time details of the plot filtered through to the English court and letters in Queen Mary's writing established that she was in support of it.

Shrewsbury was therefore ordered to remove her without delay to Sheffield Castle, his main seat, where she could be more closely guarded. On a raw November morning, in spite of her persistent pleas that she was ill, she was forced to mount a horse and make the cross country journey of fifteen miles over the hills from Baslow and crossing Totley moors to arrive, weak and exhausted, at Sheffield.

A massive stone fortress, the castle was situated at the confluence of the River Don and the River Sheaf. On a hill not far away stood Sheffield Manor surrounded by a park containing thousands of deer and used by the Shrewsbury family as a hunting lodge. It was also used as an alternative dwelling when the castle had to be cleaned and, on its flat roofed turret, Queen Mary enjoyed taking the air when she was there and watching the hunting in the park. She was no longer allowed to ride herself after the Chatsworth plot to rescue her.

For the moment however, she was so ill that Queen Elizabeth sent a letter of condolence and two of her own physicians. As she slowly recovered she found that a drastic reduction had been made in the number of her staff and more severe restrictions placed upon her movements.

Bess was constantly in Queen Mary's company and witnessed her genuine grief and distress when she learned that the Duke of Norfolk had been condemned to death. 'All bewepte and mourning', was how Bess described her as she took to her bed and refused to listen to Bess's words of consolation.

With her usual vacillation, Queen Elizabeth wavered over the signing of Norfolk's death warrant and it was not until June

1572 that he was finally executed. By this time the Scottish queen was becoming increasingly difficult to please and showed much hostility to both Bess and her husband, refusing to acknowledge that they were carrying out Queen Elizabeth's orders.

She renewed her former requests to be allowed to visit 'La Fontagne de Bogsby' as she called Buxton but met with another refusal on the grounds that the hall Shrewsbury had built there was not ready for occupation.

'What need hath she of the Buxton well?' demanded Shrewsbury but, soon after Queen Mary had been moved to Chatsworth in the summer of 1573, he was given instructions to 'carry her thither'.

Buxton was already famous as a spa where more and more people went to take the waters and Shrewsbury, for the benefit of his family and friends, had built a new residential hall close to the baths on the site of the present Old Hall Hotel. In this 'very goodlie hous, foure stories hye, a bewty to beholde', Queen Mary stayed for five weeks and took the cure daily, drinking the water and bathing in the pool while Shrewsbury was kept busy scrutinising all her visitors.

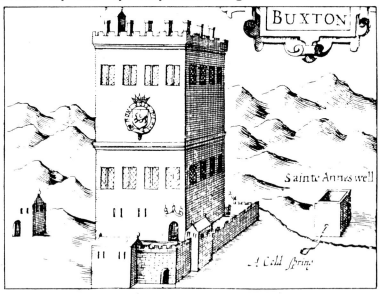

St. Anne's Well, Buxton   Speed's map of Derbyshire 1610

Bess remained at Chatsworth and, as usual when they were separated, she received most affectionate letters from the earl. 'My deare none', he addressed her, 'of all the joyes I have under God, the greatest is yourself'.

On returning to Chatsworth, a rumour that Queen Elizabeth intended to travel to Derbyshire 'there to relax herself in disguise' caused great excitement. From the time she set foot in England Queen Mary had longed to meet her 'good sister' and the Shrewsburys felt that a visit from the English Monarch would compensate for the trials they had encountered in their custodianship of Queen Mary. But the visit did not materialise and the two queens never met.

Before long, Queen Mary was again at Sheffield and, from there, she made two brief visits to Worksop Manor, another of Shrewsbury's mansions. She was also allowed three more short breaks at Buxton although Cecil, now Lord Burghley, rebuked the earl for taking her there twice in one year when Queen Elizabeth had given her consent for Queen Mary to take the waters only once. When staying at Buxton for the last time, she wrote with a diamond on her bedroom window,

'Buxton whose fame thy milk-warm waters tell,
Whom I, perchance, no more shall see, farewell'.

Guarding the Scottish queen became a full-time occupation for Bess and her husband and placed an enormous strain on their family life. The removal of the royal prisoner from one castle to another involved complicated security arrangements and, whenever the Shrewsburys moved with her, Bess had all her gold and silver plate and 'most valuable chattels' taken along as well. By degrees they found themselves cut off from their families and friends. Every member of their establishment was vetted on entering and leaving whichever castle Queen Mary was living in at the time and their sons and daughters treated in the same way.

'It seems that her majesty has no liking that our children should be with us wherever the queen is', complained the earl.

In the summer of 1574 Queen Mary's mother-in-law, the Countess of Lennox, set out from London to visit her estates in the north of England. She was accompanied by her son, Charles Stuart aged eighteen, who was Darnley's only surviving brother. Permission for this expedition had been granted on condition that they did not call at either Chatsworth or Sheffield on the way nor make any contact with Queen Mary.

On their return Bess invited them to break their journey at Rufford Abbey in Nottinghamshire, yet another of Shrewsbury's seats, presented to his father by King Henry VIII and renovated under Bess's guidance. As might be expected, Bess was at Rufford to welcome them and with her was her only unmarried daughter, the nineteen year old Elizabeth Cavendish. By a strange coincidence the Countess of Lennox became indisposed on arriving at Rufford and found it necessary to keep to her bed for several days. Bess occupied herself with looking after the invalid and kept well in the background while a love affair developed between Charles and Elizabeth.

The result, in the Countess of Lennox's words, was that 'Charles entangled himself so that he could have none other' and a speedy marriage was arranged. This took place quietly in October in the chapel at Rufford Abbey after which the two families awaited Queen Elizabeth's wrath to fall when she heard the news. Charles Stuart, like Mary Queen of Scots, was a grandchild of Henry VIII's sister and in line for the English throne. The queen's sanction was therefore required for his betrothal. Presented with a 'fait accompli', her fury knew no bounds. Shrewsbury wrote hurriedly to court with the excuse that the marriage had been 'dealt in suddenly' and without his knowledge, explaining that the young bridegroom was 'so far in love that belike he is sicke without her'. But his apologies were of no avail. The two countesses were peremptorily called to London, together with the happy couple. Elizabeth Shrewsbury and Margaret Lennox were confined in the Tower while Charles and Elizabeth were ordered to stay indoors at their house at Hackney and talk to no-one.

Bess was released early the following year and she returned to Sheffield to find that her husband was now in disgrace. Bess's daughter, Mary, the wife of Gilbert Talbot, had given birth to a son who would, presumably, be Shrewsbury's heir for his eldest son, Francis, had no children. After sending the announcement to Lord Burghley, the proud grandfather promptly received a severe rebuke from Queen Elizabeth for allowing his daughter-in-law to be confined where Mary Queen of Scots was in residence. The event might cause 'women and strangers to repair thither' he was told and, although Shrewsbury replied, assuring Her Majesty that nobody but the midwife had been granted access and he had gone so far as to christen the new-born child himself, he was ordered to reduce the number of Queen Mary's staff and to guard her more rigidly.

Together again, Bess and her husband continued their dispute about a marriage dowry for Elizabeth Stuart. Since the marriage had taken place without Shrewsbury's approval, he maintained his determination to give her nothing. Bess pleaded and argued in vain. At length, 'by brawling', she managed to get a promise of £3,000 for her daughter and, with this, she had to be satisfied. This was one of many disagreements that began to undermine their marriage and Shrewsbury's attitude to his wife became increasingly aggressive.

For the moment however, Bess's main concern was the birth of Elizabeth's baby. The Cavendish and Stuart alliance was gratifying to both grandmothers. The Countess of Lennox, released from the Tower later in the year, was constantly deploring the shortage of money in her family and welcomed a share in the Cavendish wealth. As for Bess, a country squire's daughter, the marriage was a triumph. Her future grandson would have royal blood in his veins and, already, she saw him on the throne of England.

As it turned out, the child was a girl. Probably born at Chatsworth in the autumn of 1575 though no records of the time and place of her birth exist, she was called Arbella and, according to Bess, she soon developed into 'a very proper child of great towardness'. Because of her absorbing interest in the upbringing of Arbella whose father died before she was a year old and on account of her continual supervision required for work going on at Chatsworth, Bess spent more and more time there while the earl was forced to remain in Sheffield with

Arbella Stuart at the age of 23 months
Reproduced by kind permission of The National Trust

his royal prisoner. Both husband and wife bemoaned the other's neglect.

'I see out of sight, out of mind with you', wrote Bess when complaining that Shrewsbury had failed to send timbers she had asked for. Then, with a sign of affection, she added, 'I have sent you lettuce for that you love them'.

Riding from Bolsover to Sheffield, Shrewsbury unburdened his grievances to his son, Gilbert.

'How often', he lamented, 'have I cursed the building at Chatsworth for want of her company'.

Gilbert tried to assure him that Bess's love for him was unchanged though she believed he was 'gladder of her absence than her presence'. He did his best to persuade Bess to return to Sheffield, tempting her by writing to say that his little son, George, wanted to see 'Lady Danmode'. But a few days afterwards the child died suddenly and Shrewsbury was again without an heir.

Bess was inconsolable. 'My wife', wrote Shrewsbury to Walsingham, Secretary of State, 'has driven herself into such a case by her continual weeping that I am desirous to go to her for a while'. This meant, of course, that Queen Mary had to go as well and so, in September, the usual cavalcade set out for another brief visit to Chatsworth. Once more Bess and her husband were living together but the reconciliation was of short duration.

Queen Mary, whose friendship with Bess had cooled considerably on account of the Stuart marriage, now began to take an interest in Arbella and became very fond of her until she became aware of Bess's plan for Arbella to inherit the English throne.

'Nothing has alienated the Countess from me more', she wrote indignantly to the French ambassador, 'than the vain hope she has conceived of setting the crown of England on the head of her granddaughter'.

The death of the Countess of Lennox in 1578 came as a shock to Bess and her daughter, Elizabeth, and they were shattered to learn that, after giving her an impressive funeral and a monument in Westminster Abbey, Queen Elizabeth proceeded to take possession of all the Lennox estates in England, those in Scotland having been seized after Charles Stuart's death by King James. This meant that there was nothing left for Arbella or her mother.

In the autumn of that year Bess travelled to London in order to press not only for an allowance for her daughter and granddaughter but also for the title of Countess of Lennox to be restored, this having been revoked by King James in May. The sum of £200 and £400 a year respectively was granted to Arbella and her mother but Bess considered this quite insufficient and, affronted, she returned to Sheffield.

Shrewsbury's health was now deteriorating. His temper became uncertain, his actions unpredictable. Deeply hurt by what he considered to be ill-treatment from Bess, harassed by reproaches from Queen Elizabeth and exhausted by Queen Mary's everlasting complaints and intrigues, he was also plagued by his 'old friend goute' and a 'great ache' in his wrists which caused difficulty in writing. Gilbert found his father 'in exceeding choler of slight occasion' and, indeed, the state of Shrewsbury's finances at that time was enough to exacerbate his mental state. While never losing sight of the fact that his royal prisoner might one day occupy the throne of England, he was now beginning to resent the burden of his custodianship and its annual drain on his resources.

Fixed originally at £52 a week, his allowance for the Scottish queen and her household was soon reduced to £30 and this amount was paid very irregularly. In a letter to Burghley, begging for an increase, Shrewsbury protested that the funds he received would not cover the cost of food for his own servants. He criticised the quantity of food and drink consumed by Queen Mary's attendants 'on fishe dayes and fleshe dayes', the gentlemen being supplied with eight dishes at each meal and the ladies with five. The wine, spice and fuel used in his house, he asserted, 'cometh not under £1,000 by the year'. It was estimated that, at Wingfield, 2,520 gallons of wine were got through annually as Queen Mary used it for baths. Between the queen and his wife, lamented Shrewsbury, he was being reduced to a 'pencyoner'.

In 1582 the family faced two tragedies. In the New Year Bess's daughter, Elizabeth, died at Sheffield and, in August, Shrewsbury's eldest son, Francis Talbot, was a victim of the plague in London. 'My wife', wrote Shrewsbury, 'taketh her daughter Lennox's death so grieviously that she cannot think of aught but tears'. He also supported Bess's many subsequent requests for an increase in 'the poor orphan's' income but to these Queen Elizabeth turned a deaf ear.

Nevertheless, Bess spared no expense in the upbringing of 'My Jewel' as she called Arbella, ever conscious that her granddaughter might one day be the Queen of England. Arbella had her own attendants and, for her education, Bess appointed the most highly qualified tutors. Lessons in music, dancing, Latin and Greek continued when the child stayed with her aunt, Mary Talbot, and with other relatives and, at the age of seven, she was able to compose an excellent letter in French.

Francis Talbot died leaving many debts and, as he had no children, Gilbert became Shrewsbury's heir but was unpopular with his father because he championed Bess's cause.

In the following year Bess bought her old home, Hardwick Hall, from her brother, James, who died, bankrupt in the Fleet prison. The purchase price was £9,500 and was made in the name of Bess's second son, William Cavendish who was knighted in 1580 and became the first Earl of Devonshire in 1618.

Shrewsbury now made it clear that he would not have Bess under his roof again. He cut off her allowance of £800 a year and appropriated revenues from lands which had officially been made over to William and Charles Cavendish. The latter, who was knighted in 1582, was the victim of an attack by a party of the earl's servants at Ashford-in-the-Water when he had to seek sanctuary in the church for safety and was 'forced to take to the Steeple'. Continuing the persecution of his wife, Shrewsbury sent men to harass the tenants at Chatsworth in order to get from them rents which were due to Bess. Finally, arriving at Chatsworth House with forty mounted men, he demanded entrance on the grounds that he was the owner, causing Bess to flee to Hardwick.

In spite of her husband's animosity, Bess continued to write to him, frequently, expressing grief at their separation and pleading to be reconciled and restored as his wife. She would do nothing, she assured him, 'but it shall be for your honour and good'. But now Shrewsbury was almost paronoid in his hatred, calling her 'that sharp and bitter shrew' and declaring that he was 'ashamed of his choice of such a creature'. In vain the Bishop of Coventry and Lichfield reminded him that 'if shrewishness and sharpness be a just cause for separation, I think that few men in England would keep their wives for long'.

But Shrewsbury remained implacable. 'I try all I can to be rid of this troublesome burden', he told his friends, most of whose sympathies lay with Bess.

Both families, Talbots and Cavendishes, were also on Bess's side with the exception of her eldest son, Henry Cavendish. He and his wife, Grace, had failed to produce an heir although he had a host of illegitimate offspring and was known as 'the common bull of Derbyshire and Staffordshire'.

Permanently in debt, he borrowed from his mother and from Shrewsbury and sold many of his properties in Nottinghamshire that Bess had bought for him.

It will never be known who was responsible for the wild rumour that now began to circulate concerning a liaison between Mary, Queen of Scots and her custodian, Shrewsbury. Suspicion that Bess and her sons were the instigators was never verified but Queen Mary had no doubt that Bess was the culprit. A reply given by Bess, when asked by Queen Elizabeth how the Scottish queen fared, might have contained a hint that she was aware of some mutual attraction.

'Madame', she said, 'she cannot do ill while she is with my husband and I begin to grow jealous; they are so great together'.

When even more scandalous reports swept through the country to the effect that Queen Mary had borne a child of Shrewsbury's (and some said two), the distressed Queen of Scots begged to be allowed to go to court in order to vindicate herself. As she received no reply from London, she wrote a startling letter to Queen Elizabeth in which she exposed Bess's treachery in promising to help her to escape and hinted that she could reveal 'other features' of Bess's misconduct. Writing 'without passion and with true sincerity', she revealed how Bess had described incidents at court when Queen Elizabeth's ladies had mocked the queen for her vanity and had been shocked by their sovereign's alleged immoral practices with Leicester and other men at court.

It is unlikely that Her Majesty ever set eyes on this missive for it was found, after her death, among papers belonging to Lord Burghley.

Shrewsbury also begged for permission to see Queen Elizabeth and clear himself of 'these venomous accusations'. His request was granted. The queen received him graciously and he was officially exonerated of any unseemly conduct with the Queen of Scots. Her Majesty took this opportunity to discuss the earl's marriage and ordered him to take Bess back into his house and 'treat her with courtesy'. Grudgingly, he allowed her to 'share his roof' at Wingfield but their temporary reunion was no more than a facade and, within a short time, they separated for good.

'I could not be contented to accept of you', wrote the earl to his wife' 'till you did confess upon your knees that you had offended me'.

Not prepared to humble herself in such a manner, Bess refused.

Soon afterwards Shrewsbury was relieved of his guardianship of Queen Mary and he thanked Queen Elizabeth for thereby setting him free from two devils, his wife and the Queen of Scots.

On the Duke of Norfolk's death, Shrewsbury had succeeded him as Earl Marshal of England and he was therefore required to be present when Queen Mary was tried at Fotheringay Castle as a result of the Babington Plot. At her execution on 8th February 1587 it was his duty to raise his baton of office as a signal to the executioner to make the fatal stroke with his axe. Three blows were needed before the royal head was finally severed and, as Queen Mary's little Skye terrier crept from beneath her blood-stained skirts, Shrewsbury turned away his face and wept.

Bess now divided her time between Hardwick and Wingfield and made it clear that, at any time, she would be pleased to live 'in house' with her husband again. But, in spite of a cordial letter from Queen Elizabeth in which she urged the earl to see his wife occasionally, 'which she hath now a long time wanted', he continued to harbour bitter feelings against Bess and took refuge at Handsworth Manor near Sheffield where he was consoled by Mrs Eleanor Britton, a lady of his household.

Shrewsbury's health declined rapidly and he died on 18th November 1590 after forecasting that Arbella Stuart would be the source of much trouble to Bess and her family. His funeral, on a cold January day in the following year, was a magnificent spectacle attended by some 20,000 people, 'both of nobility, gentry and country folks'. His tomb had been prepared before his death and so had the elegy of twenty-three verses inscribed on it. This makes no mention of Bess but gives details of his public services and includes the lines,

'Soe great a trust as this was never seene,
A subject for to be a keeper of a Queen'.

Gilbert Talbot, now the 7th Earl of Shrewsbury and hoping to inherit enough to pay his long-standing debts, was shattered to find that his father had left so little money. The drain on the 6th earl's income had been caused by his long custody of Mary Queen of Scots, by huge family expenses and, latterly, by Eleanor Britton who had appropriated for herself and her son a large amount of gold and jewels. Following Shrewsbury's death, she put in a claim for lands and cattle as well.

After several quarrels with Gilbert, Bess got possession of all the properties to which she was entitled under the marriage settlement. Together with Wingfield Manor she received iron and glass works, with Bolsover, presented to her husband by Edward VI, came the collieries and from numerous lands in Staffordshire and Yorkshire as well as Derbyshire, timber and minerals could be obtained to add to her wealth. Her income was now about £60,000 a year.

Still full of vitality and enjoying robust health only marred by an occasional touch of rheumatism, Bess was now free to move around her estates at her own convenience. However, since Chatsworth was entailed on her eldest son, Henry Cavendish, and Wingfield was Talbot property, the only house she owned outright was Hardwick and this she set about rebuilding for her favourite son, William.

Called an architectural hotch-potch, the Old Hall was designed as the alterations went along, wings and extra floors being added haphazardly when found necessary. A suite of state apartments was situated inconveniently on the top floor and the newly built kitchens had the appearance of being in danger of slipping over into the valley.

Long before Shrewsbury's death Bess had plans drawn up by Robert Smythson for a new hall at Hardwick and, at the beginning of November, 1590, its foundations were dug within a stone's throw of the Old Hall. Within twelve months the walls had reached the second floor but here the work stopped temporarily for, in the autumn of 1591, Bess made her last journey to London.

After months of preparations, the party set out in November 1591. Among the retinue of forty which accompanied her were Bess's sons, William and Charles Cavendish, with their wives, her granddaughter, Arbella Stuart and her attendants, together with ladies and gentlemen-in-waiting, household servants, brewers, cooks and kitchen staff. The ladies travelled in two large lumbering coaches, the rest of the party on horseback. Footmen running ahead to each town on the route gave notice of the Countess's approach so that church bells could be rung, accommodation prepared and stabling found for the horses. At each stopping place crowds of poor people waited for coins to be thrown to them and sightseers gathered to see the cavalcade. The journey took seven days.

Sheep and oxen to be slaughtered for food had been driven from Bess's estates in Leicestershire and furniture and hangings from Derbyshire were transported to add to those in Shrewsbury House at Chelsea in what is now Cheyne Walk. Situated by the River Thames, the house was easily accessible for the delivery of provisions and for visitors arriving by boat.

Soon after their arrival, a massive shopping expedition took place when yards of exotic materials were bought to be made into gowns for the Christmas celebrations at Whitehall. Bess spent £300 on clothes which included black taffeta and 'cobweb lawn' to be made into dresses for herself and velvets and satins for Arbella.

Bess and her family were received graciously by Queen Elizabeth but there are no reports of Arbella's part in the festivities although she commented afterwards, 'What fair words I have had of courtiers and councillors, and so they are vanished in smoke'.

This was Arbella's third visit to Court. In August 1587 Queen Elizabeth had sent for the twelve year old girl and treated her with kindness.

'Look at her well', said Her Majesty, 'for one day she will be even as I am'.

The following year, Arbella was again at Court but this time her behaviour was overweening. After the death of Mary Queen of Scots which brought Arbella one step nearer the throne, Bess had insisted that the girl should be treated as a princess of royal blood, her relatives being ordered to curtsey to her and address her as 'Highness'. As a result, Arbella insisted on taking precedence over Queen Elizabeth's ladies which caused Her Majesty to order sharply that she was to be escorted back to Derbyshire.

Now, however, under the wing of her grandmother, she was more subdued and she accompanied Bess to Greenwich Palace for a stay over Whitsuntide. When Bess departed for Hardwick on July 31st 1592, Arbella was invited to remain at Court, thus raising Bess's hopes afresh that her granddaughter might be named as Queen Elizabeth's successor.

During the spring, Bess had made further purchases of gold and silver plate, pictures and tapestries for her new Hall and these included the seventeen hangings showing the story of Gideon, still to be seen in the Long Gallery at Hardwick. In the eight months of her visit to London, Bess spent £6,360.

For her journey home, Bess bought a new and very costly litter, upholstered in velvet with windows of gold parchment and a felt covered footstool. Travelling in this up-to-date conveyance slung between four horses, Bess set out for Derbyshire followed by her retinue on forty-three hired horses and by ten great wagons which contained her purchases. Before reaching Nottingham, Bess left the rest of the party in order to spend a night at Holme Pierrepont with her eldest daughter, Frances, and granddaughter, Grace, who was soon to marry Dorothy Vernon's son, George Manners and become the ancestor of the Dukes of Rutland.

From there she visited her friend, Sir Francis Willoughby, at Wollaton Hall and agreed to lend him £3,000, the security being five of his manors, with an interest of £300 to be paid to Arbella Stuart.

Bess returned to Hardwick to find that the Old Hall had been made more habitable in her absence and she settled down to supervise the resumption of work on the new Hall. During her visit to London stone had been quarried on the Hardwick estate and 'dressed' ready for building which now advanced rapidly.

Within a few weeks of Bess's return, Arbella joined her at Hardwick and shortly afterwards a letter arrived from

Burghley, warning Bess to keep a close watch on her grand-daughter as a plot to kidnap her was suspected. Bess wrote in reply, promising to look out for any suspicious characters.

'Arbel', she assured Lord Burghley, 'walks not late. I see her almost every hour of the day. She lieth in my bedchamber'.

Nevertheless, she decided to take Arbella to Chatsworth for greater security.

Early in 1593 they were back at Hardwick when Bess began negotiations for purchasing the manors of Heath, Stainsby and Owlcotes*. The transaction completed, she immediately put in hand the building of a new house at Owlcotes* for William who still had no home of his home and occupied apartments in the Old Hall at Hardwick

Work on the new Hall continued apace with building materials brought from all parts of Derbyshire. Sandstone came from the quarries at Hardwick, lime from Skegby and Crich and alabaster from Tutbury. The famous black marble was produced at Ashford and lead for the roof and spouts was brought from the lands at Barlow that Bess had inherited from her first husband. Teams of oxen dragged timber from Chatsworth Park and from Heath and Stainsby but much of it was used, unseasoned, and as a result, many of the floors are uneven to this day.

Regularly Bess inspected the progress of the building, strictly overlooking the workmen and keeping a careful watch on the accounts which were meticulously kept and still survive.

The highest paid workman was Abraham Smith, a mason, plasterer and carpenter, who had worked for Bess at Chatsworth. His half-yearly pay was £6.13.4 and his keep, together with the tenancy of a smallholding at Ashford. In June 1591 building was going on at both the old and new halls, employing over fifty labourers at sixpence a day. They were recruited from nearby Hardstoft and Tibshelf but many came from as far away as Chesterfield. A man who had trudged for miles to find work at Hardwick arrived barefoot and in rags and was given an advance of his wages to buy shoes. The men were provided with food and those coming

* Known as Oldcotes today

from a distance slept in the 'workfolks' chamber' or within the building itself. In summertime they spent their nights in the fields or under hedges. Local women were employed in carrying water and mixing plaster but they earned only one penny a day. By the time alterations were complete in the Old Hall and the building of the New hall was finished, the estimated cost for labour alone was £5,000.

As the hall was nearing completion, Bess turned her attention to charity and gave orders for the erection of two almshouses, one at Bakewell and one in Full Street, Derby. The latter accommodated twelve poor persons of the town who were instructed to attend a church service twice daily and offer prayers for 'our noble founder'. The penalty for neglecting to do this was twopence.

On October 4th 1597 Bess took up residence, with her granddaughter, Arbella, in the new Hardwick Hall. Four musicians 'played them in' but, at the same time, work was still going on and continued for two more years.

Called by an eighteenth century writer, 'one of the proudest piles ever beheld', the magnificent house stands indomitably on the crest of a hill surrounded by parkland. Built in perfect all round symmetry with its six towers, each one hundred feet high, its outstanding feature is the size of the windows which increase in height on each successive floor and contain a vast amount of glass, in itself, a status symbol in Elizabethan times. 'Hardwick Hall, more glass than wall', was consequently a very cold place to live in.

On the skyline, Bess's initials, E.S., surmounted by a coronet, are repeated all round the crenelations and catch the eye from every direction.

Life at Hardwick resembled that of a minor court. Bess at the centre was surrounded by her family and by upper and lower servants who all wore a pale blue livery. The upper servants usually belonged to good families and were known as gentlewomen and gentlemen, the latter looking after the estate with Timothy Pusey at their head. He submitted the household accounts to Bess each week and she signed them, 'E. Shroesbury'.

The gentlewomen, all given the title of Mrs, were under the

Hardwick Hall. © John N. Merrill

supervision of Mrs Digby, Bess's chief companion and assistant. They helped to look after Bess's family and guests, important visitors being entertained in the Great High Chamber on the second floor. With its plaster frieze of forest scenes, created by Abraham Smith, it has been described as the most beautiful room in the whole of Europe. It was here that meals were served on state occasions. Food was brought up from the kitchens by a procession of servants for dinner at 11am and supper between 5 and 6pm. Afterwards dancing took place and plays and masques were produced.

The gallery, 166 feet long and 20 feet high, which took up half the second floor, was a reception room for distinguished guests and was used for exercise in bad weather. On the walls were hung the Gideon tapestries and portraits of Bess and her family as well as of royal personages.

As there were only fourteen principal bedrooms, any overflow of guests had to be accommodated in the Old Hall and here the upper servants had their own rooms. The lower servants slept on straw pallets, rolled up in the daytime, on landings and in corridors, within call whenever they were needed. Their meals were taken with the workmen in the hall on the ground floor where the kitchens and nurseries were also situated.

All the cleaning and cooking was done by men, the women servants being employed as ladies' maids, laundry maids or children's nurses for William Cavendish and his family spent a great deal of time at Hardwick.

Bedrooms had close stools of which the contents were carried downstairs and emptied into one of the outside privies. Bess had her own little closet off her bedchamber where a close stool was 'covered with blewe cloth stitcht in white with red and black silke fringe'.

Every room depended for warmth and light on open fires and candles. Water was pumped from a well in the grounds and carried into the house through a pipe of lead.

The embroidered bed hangings in the Queen of Scots room, with its cipher M.R. and the royal arms of Scotland over the door, may have been worked by the Scottish queen herself but she was never in residence there nor is there any evidence that she ever stayed at the Old Hall.

Now she was settled in a fitting home for a possible future queen of England, Bess might have looked forward to spending the peace of old age in what was to be her most enduring monument. Instead, she was constantly harassed by the reckless conduct of her lively, wayward granddaughter.

Arbella was twenty-two when, along with her grandmother, she moved into the new Hardwick Hall and, for some years, she had been causing Bess no little anxiety.

'She has very exalted ideas', stated a contemporary writer, 'having been brought up in the firm belief that she would succeed to the crown'.

Out of favour at Queen Elizabeth's court on account of her overbearing manner, she spent her days either in impatient boredom at Hardwick or with the family of her aunt, Mary Talbot, who had become a Roman Catholic. Mary was therefore 'in bad conceit' with Her Majesty who soon ordered Arbella to remain at Hardwick with Bess where she was virtually a prisoner.

Described as 'sufficiently handsome in the face', Arbella was a quick witted, vivacious girl, desperately anxious to find a husband as she believed that marriage meant freedom. Various suitors had been suggested for her but none was approved by Queen Elizabeth so Arbella set about making her own plans and managed to enlist the help of Henry Cavendish who was always eager to thwart his mother.

John Dodderidge, an old man employed by Bess, was persuaded to take a message to the Earl of Hertford in London, asking the earl to arrange for his sixteen year old grandson, Edward Seymour, to visit Hardwick in disguise so that Arbella could look him over as a prospective bridegroom. On a horse provided by Henry Cavendish, Dodderidge reluctantly made the journey and dutifully delivered the message.

Hertford, whose ill-fated marriage to Catherine Grey had brought about the imprisonment in the Tower of his wife, himself and Bess as well, was hardly likely to risk his sovereign's wrath a second time by consenting to Arbella's union with Edward, both having royal blood in their veins. He therefore lost no time in sending Dodderidge to court where he was questioned carefully and then put in the Gatehouse Jail by Sir Robert Cecil, Burghley's son, who was now the queen's secretary.

At Hardwick a few days later the unexpected appearance of Sir Henry Bronker, a queen's commissioner, filled Bess with apprehension. Sir Henry was received in the Long Gallery where Bess was walking with Arbella and William Cavendish and he hastened to convey to her a gracious message from the queen which temporarily dispelled her fears.

He then contrived to draw Arbella to the far end of the gallery where, with a written confession from Dodderidge in his pocket, he then demanded that she explain her behaviour. But Arbella denied everything and made a number of contradictory statements in which she declared that Dodderidge was a 'lewd, bold fellow' and would do anything for gain. Bronker then asked her to make a written account of the facts which she gave him the following morning but this, he protested, was 'confused, obscure and, in truth, ridiculous'. He then proceeded to write down his own findings of the situation, commenting that Arbella's 'wits were somewhat distracted', and prepared to return to London. Before his departure he felt bound to disclose details of the affair to Bess, leaving Arbella to her Grandmother's fury and the realisation that, in attempting to become betrothed without the queen's approval, she was guilty of treason.

Bess lost no time in writing to Queen Elizabeth and denying any knowledge of her granddaughter's harebrained plan. She begged Her Majesty to place Arbella 'elsewhere or to bestow her in marriage'. An unsatisfactory reply from the queen suggested only that Arbella should remain at Hardwick and be closely watched.

So, for the time-being the ageing countess and the twenty-seven year old girl kept an uneasy truce. Arbella was forbidden to ride and her visitors were restricted but she continued to torment her grandmother with threats to escape and hints that she had a secret lover. Fearing that Arbella's mind was becoming unbalanced, Bess asked that Sir Henry Bronker might pay another visit to Hardwick.

'Arbell is so wilfully bent', she wrote, 'that she hath made a vow not to eat or drink in this house. I am weary of my life', she added, pathetically, and this brought Sir Henry post-haste from London once more. But he found it impossible to carry on a reasonable discussion with Arbella who reiterated that she meant to have her liberty and refused to name her alleged suitor. He returned to London, leaving Bess in a distressed state and, in desperation, she wrote to Sir Robert Cecil. She implored him to obtain the queen's permission for Arbella to leave Hardwick.

'A few weeks more as I have suffered will make an end of me', she declared.

Heated arguments and angry words shattered the peace of Hardwick and, finally, an attempt to abduct Arbella was made by Henry Cavendish who arrived at the gates with forty armed horsemen. Messages were carried back and forth between Bess and her 'bad son', as she called him but, in the end, Arbella was persuaded not to go with him and Bess sent, once again, for Bronker.

On this, his third visit, he realised the gravity of the situation. He now began to doubt Arbella's sanity and, on his recommendation, she was at last removed from her grandmother's care. She was taken to Wrest Park in Bedfordshire, the home of the Earl of Kent whose nephew had married Elizabeth, daughter of Gilbert and Mary Talbot. Bess was now left in peace and, for company, she was pleased to have her favourite sister, Jane Kniveton, who was given her own apartments in the Hall.

Meantime, at the Palace of Richmond, Queen Elizabeth lay dying. With a nod she indicated, on her death bed, that James VI of Scotland should succeed her and, on 24th March 1603, she died.

On his journey from Scotland to London, King James stayed one night with the Earl and Countess of Shrewsbury at Worksop Manor and was 'magnificently entertained'. But Bess took no part in the celebrations. Her dreams for Arbella had finally faded and she set about making preparations for her own death.

In 1601 Bess had made a will leaving Hardwick Hall and Owlcotes to William and the contents of Chatsworth House to Henry who, as the eldest son, would inherit the house and estate. To Arbella, her 'very loving granddaughter', she left £1,000 in money, most of her pearls and jewels, her sable and a 'christal glasse set with Lapis Lazarus and Aggett'. But Arbella's disgraceful behaviour and Henry's encouragement of it caused her to add a codicil two years later revoking everything she had bequeathed to them in her will.

She also made a detailed inventory of the Hall's contents, listing every piece of furniture, linen and embroidery, every article of gold or silver, all hangings, featherbeds, ticks and chamberpots and each utensil used in the kitchens.

She paid a visit to All Hallows' Church in Derby and purchased from the bailiffs and burgesses a site for her vault at the east end of the south aisle. She ordered her effigy to be made in alabaster so that it 'wanted nothing but setting up' and she directed that her funeral be 'not too sumptuous'.

Arbella, 'still without mate and without estate', was now living at the court of her cousin, King James, and was on friendly terms with Queen Anne. In 1605 she made a journey

Bess of Hardwick's Memorial in Derby Cathedral.
Photograph by John N. Merrill.

to Hardwick, carrying the news that William was to be made Baron Cavendish of Hardwick. As William was Bess's favourite son, this act contributed to Arbella's being forgiven her past misconduct.

After the Gunpowder Plot late that year instructions were sent to the Derbyshire justices requiring them to be 'vigilant in the protection of Lady Shrewsbury, Dowager' and to 'have a care of her safety and quietness'. By this time, however, Bess took little interest in what occurred outside Hardwick. Her health was beginning to fail though her mind remained wonderfully alert.

Although the Earl and Countess of Shrewsbury had been out of favour with her for some time, they now made a ceremonial visit to Hardwick in order to be reconciled. Charles Cavendish arrived at the same time and all were received 'with respect and affection'.

'We found', wrote Gilbert, describing the visit, 'a lady of great years, of great wealth and of great wit', but, to his brother-in-law, Henry Cavendish, he confessed, 'She did eat little and was not able to walk the length of the chamber'.

The winter of 1607 to 1608 was exceptionally cold when rivers in Derbyshire became solid ice and birds fell, frozen, from the trees. The legend that Bess would continue to live until she stopped building and that she gave orders for workmen to use boiling ale instead of water to mix the mortar has little foundation in fact for at that time no building was in progress.

On 2nd February 1608 Dr. Hunton from Sheffield moved to Hardwick in order to be in constant attention on his illustrious patient. Dosed with treacle from time to time, Bess lay in her four-poster bed with its scarlet and gold curtains for eleven days and nights as she quietly waited for death. Members of her family and household dropped in occasionally to pay their last respects and on 13th February 'at about five of the clock' Elizabeth, Countess of Shrewsbury, drew her last breath. Her body was embalmed and she lay in state for three months while arrangements for her funeral were made.

Sometime in May the procession set out from Hardwick, taking Bess on her last journey. Swarms of sightseers lined the roads and, when the cortège arrived in Derby, the town witnessed appalling scenes of drunkenness and brawling with crowds clamouring for the customary funeral dole.

The ceremony took place with due pomp in what is now the cathedral. The coffin, draped in black, was followed by Bess's daughter, Mary, Countess of Shrewsbury, as chief mourner and many other members of her family. It is not known whether or not Arbella Stuart was present but Henry Cavendish and Gilbert, Earl of Shrewsbury, did not attend. The Archbishop of York preached the funeral sermon and Bess was interred in the vault she had bought for herself where, later, she was joined by more than forty of her descendants.

Shrewsbury

'When Hardwick's towers shall bow their head,
Nor mass be more in Worksop said,
When Bolsover's fair fame shall tend
Like Oldcotes, to its mouldering end,
When Chatsworth tastes no Ca'endish bounties,
Let fame forget this costly countess'.

Horace Walpole. 1760

SOURCES

Bess of Hardwick	David N. Durant
Bess of Hardwick	E. Carleton Williams
Mistress of Hardwick	Alison Plowden
Hardwick Hall	Mark Girouard
Hardwick Hall	The National Trust
The Building of Hardwick Hall	David N. Durant and Philip Riden
Derbyshire	Roy Christian
Derbyshire	Arthur Mee
Derbyshire	T. L. Tudor
Derbyshire Guide	Derbyshire Countryside Ltd.
Derbyshire Characters	Derbyshire Countryside Ltd.
Bygone Derbyshire	William Andrews
Historic Buildings of Derbyshire	John Merrill
Companion into Derbyshire	E. Carleton Williams
History of Derby	John Heath
History Of Sheffield	J. E. Vickers
Nottinghamshire	Roy Christian
Wingfield Manor	W. H. Edmunds
Tutbury Castle	Duchy of Lancaster
Chatsworth	F. Thompson
The House	The Duchess of Devonshire
Mary Queen of Scots	Antonia Fraser
The Captive Queen in Derbyshire	Elizabeth Eisenberg
Arbella Stuart	David N. Durant
Queen Elizabeth	J. E. Neale
Life and Times of Queen Elizabeth	N. Williams
Buildings of England	Nicolas Pevsner
Dictionary of National Biography	
Derbyshire Archaeological Society Journals	
Bygone Derbyshire	

Illustrations on pages 8 and 16 are taken from
'Palaces, Prisons and resting Places of Mary Queen of Scots'

Other Related Books in this Series:

'Tudor Derbyshire'
Gives a background of Derbyshire during the period

'The Water Cure'
Covers the Spa at Buxton visited by Mary Queen of Scots

' Manors and Families of Derbyshire'
Includes monographs & coats of arms for Bolsover, Chatsworth, Codnor Castle, Hardwick, and Wingfield

'The Captive Queen'
Deals with the imprisonment of Mary Queen of Scots in the County

'Derbyshire Churches'
Includes All Saints Church Derby where Bess is buried, and Edensor the Chatsworth village church